20

Everything You Need to Know About

LOOKING AND FEELING YOUR BEST

A Guide for Guys

Good grooming helps to create a positive self-image.

• THE NEED TO KNOW LIBRARY •

Everything You Need to Know About

LOOKING AND FEELING YOUR BEST

A Guide for Guys

Michael A. Sommers

THE ROSEN PUBLISHING GROUP, INC.
NEW YORK

Published in 2000 by The Rosen Publishing Group, Inc.
29 East 21st Street, New York, NY 10010

Copyright © 2000 by The Rosen Publishing Group, Inc.

Revised Edition 2000

Library of Congress Cataloging-in-Publication Data

Sommers, Michael A., 1966–
    Everything you need to know about looking and feeling your best : a guide for guys / Michael A. Sommers. — Rev. ed.
      p. cm. — (The need to know library)
    Includes bibliographical references and index.
    Summary: Explains the importance of good grooming and hygiene and how they relate to the challenges of being an adolescent male.
    ISBN 0-8239-3080-7
    1. Beauty, Personal—Juvenile literature.   2. Teenage boys—Health and hygiene—Juvenile literature. [1. Boys—Health and hygiene 2. Grooming.] I. Title. II. Series.
RA777.2.S66 1999
613'.04233—dc21   99-29091
                                                       CIP

Manufactured in the United States of America

Contents

Introduction

*F*ourteen-year-old Raphael didn't understand high school at all. Last year in junior high, he had been a pretty popular guy. He had played drums in a punk band with his best friends, Raul, Zoë, and Rocco. Everybody at school thought he was cool. Guys were always high-fiving him in the halls, and girls used to slide notes into his locker. He didn't care that his parents thought his mohawk was ugly or that his teachers stared at his pierced eyebrow.

Then, over the summer, his parents separated. Raphael moved with his mother to a new neighborhood. When Raphael began high school, he didn't know anybody. When he walked down the hall in his army boots and ripped T-shirts, guys stared at him like he was a freak. Girls whispered and looked away. One teacher told him not to come to class until he had gotten a proper haircut. Another teacher acted as if he wasn't even in the classroom.

Raphael began to feel like an outsider at school. After school was just as bad. He had no friends and no band to play in anymore. He went straight home every day and pigged out on junk food in front of the television. His mother would get home late from her new job and yell at him. "Why don't you help around the house instead of just sitting around?" she would shout.

Raphael was putting on a lot of weight. After all, he never exercised. One day, he looked at himself in the mirror and was disgusted by his reflection. The boy staring back at him was pudgy. His hair was a mess and his skin was pale and unhealthy looking. He had zits and blackheads on his face and unshaved stubble on his upper lip.

Because everyone around him—his mother, his teachers, and his classmates—seemed to see him as a loser, Raphael began to think of himself as someone with no future. He stopped doing his homework and barely studied for tests. What was the point?

Since there was no reason to be in school if he wasn't prepared for his classes, Raphael began ditching school. He hung out at the ravine where he smoked cigarettes. When he could get some, he smoked marijuana. His eyes were often bloodshot. He caught people giving him wary looks in the street. At school, there were rumors that he was a messed-up druggie.

Twice, he was confronted by police officers at the

ravine. They made him empty his pockets. The first time, he only had a pack of cigarettes. But the second time, he had two joints. Raphael ended up with a juvenile police record and was suspended from school. His mother was ready to kick him out of the house. He was only allowed to return to school on the condition that he enter a counseling program. Both Raphael and his counselor decided that Raphael had to make some big changes in his life, changes that would allow himself and others to see him in a new, postive light.

Chapter 1

Good Grooming

Good grooming begins the moment your parents first bring you home from the hospital. Part of a parent's responsibility is to bathe and dress his or her children, to make sure they are clean and neatly dressed. As you grow older, little by little, parents allow you to take responsibility for your own grooming. They teach you how to scrub behind your ears and brush your teeth after meals. They help you choose the clothes you wear to school.

Unfortunately, some parents don't pay attention to how they look or what they wear. This makes it difficult for their kids to learn good grooming habits. Other parents overemphasize neatness and cleanliness. When their kids become older, they sometimes rebel against what they see as their parents' excessiveness. They might refuse to brush their hair or take regular showers. They might wear sloppy T-shirts, jeans with holes, or beat-up sneakers.

Once you grow older, especially in your teenage years, your peers have a much greater influence over the way you look, dress, talk, and act. Adolescence is a period of great change. It is a time when you start searching for your own identity. You will probably experiment with different looks in order to find a style that suits you.

Sometimes, you will want to find a look that impresses others, especially people your own age. You want to be attractive, cool, popular—you want to fit in. Often, the way to do this is by wearing a certain trendy brand of clothing or a hairstyle that is considered "in." You find that for both you and your friends, clothing and fashion suddenly become much more important. Advertising and television, athletes and models, movie stars and magazines—all of these things can influence the way you and your friends want to look and act.

At the same time, you want to assert your independence, especially with respect to your parents. You might do so by purposely choosing a look that distinguishes you from other people—one that makes you stand out from the crowd.

Ultimately, what is important is that you choose a look or style that makes you feel comfortable. The look you choose will not only reflect the person you want to be, but the way you want others to see you as well. Certain trends can be fun to follow, but you should never feel pressured to adopt them if you don't feel they are really "you." Remember that the image you choose to project can say a lot about the kind of person you are.

Feeling Fit

A lot of people think good grooming is the same as personal hygiene. But it means much more than being neat and clean and dressing well. Good grooming is about taking care of yourself in every sense. And taking care of yourself means maintaining a positive lifestyle that will keep both your body and mind as healthy as possible.

Being physically fit is one important aspect of a positive lifestyle. Exercise can—and should—be fun. Aside from making you physically healthy, physical activity gives you a sense of accomplishment. Having a healthy body makes you feel good about yourself. It is a part of being attractive—to both yourself and others.

Diet is just as important as exercise. As the saying goes, "You are what you eat." What you put into your body not only affects the way you look but also the way you move, think, and feel. These days, people are much more aware of what is nutritionally good to eat and what is not, and in what quantity. As a general rule, it is best to eat in moderation. Eating a lot of junk food is bad for your body and often leads to health problems.

The dangers of drinking, smoking, and doing drugs are widely known. Although it is common for teens to want to experiment with alcohol, tobacco, and other drugs, don't feel pressured to try them because your peers do. Even if at first it seems that drugs or alcohol make you feel good, remember that they are addictive substances that can cause serious health problems.

An activity such as yoga can make you feel better, both physically and mentally.

A State of Mind

When you feel good about yourself, it is more likely that you will achieve your goals. Think of yourself as a machine. If you are a machine that is clean, oiled, and well cared for, you will perform tasks more efficiently than a machine that is rusty, dusty, and neglected.

The history final was scheduled for Wednesday morning at 9:00 AM. The night before, Ilya studied until 9:30 PM. Then he did some relaxing tai chi exercises and went to bed at 10:30 PM.

Ilya woke up at 6:30 AM. He had time to do some push-ups and sit-ups, which left him wide awake. Then he took a long, hot shower. He took time to eat a nutritious breakfast of orange juice, oatmeal, and bananas, before taking an energetic walk to school. He arrived at school at 8:45 AM, with plenty of time to look over his notes and wait for the exam to begin.

Meanwhile, instead of studying, Moses spent Tuesday evening watching MTV at his friend Lou's house. They ate chips and pizza, and Lou even broke out some of his dad's beer. Although Moses planned to review for the test before going to bed, by the time he got home, he was feeling slightly drunk. He decided to go to bed and wake up early to study instead.

In the morning, Moses was so tired that he didn't hear his alarm clock. When he finally got up, it was 8:30 AM! He didn't have time to study, take a shower, or even eat breakfast. Hungry, hungover, and still wearing yesterday's wrinkled clothes, Moses ran all the way to school. But by the time he arrived, huffing and puffing, the exam had already begun. Moses had to take it anyway and didn't have enough time to finish.

Who do you think did better on the exam—Ilya or Moses?

The Man in the Mirror

Sometimes, it's interesting to take a good long look at yourself in the mirror. It has nothing to do with being vain. Study your face, your hair, and your posture. Are you happy with what you see?

Think about the things you like about yourself. And

then think about the things that you don't like. How can you change your lifestyle to make yourself look better and feel better? Using a toothpaste with baking soda could help to make your teeth whiter. Then you would feel inclined to smile more often. Finding a good dandruff shampoo could get rid of embarrassing flakes and allow you to wear cool, dark-colored clothes. Sitting up straight and doing back exercises might help to improve your posture. By doing so, you would feel taller and more confident about your body.

Most appearance problems have easy solutions. Often, all it takes is the desire and discipline to change, coupled with advice and help from parents or professionals. Just remember that change doesn't happen overnight. Be patient and try to set realistic goals.

Chapter 2

Good Hygiene

Personal hygiene is about cleaning and taking care of your body. Cleanliness is one of the basics of good grooming. Being near someone who doesn't bathe enough or take care of himself or herself properly is very unpleasant.

As you enter adolescence, your body changes in ways that make cleanliness an increasingly important part of your life. Glands develop that release oil and sweat. A buildup of oil in your pores can produce pimples or blackheads. Sweat is the fluid that your body releases to help you cool down, but when sweat dries on your skin or clothes, it can sometimes smell bad.

In order to keep you and your clothes looking and smelling good, it is important to take a daily bath or shower. Using soap that contains a moisturizer is a good idea because it keeps your skin from drying out.

Using a washcloth or bath brush is also good for getting rid of dead skin cells.

After drying yourself off, safeguard against body odor by using a deodorant or antiperspirant. Deodorants cover up natural odors with artificial ones. Antiperspirants contain a chemical that actually soaks up sweat, keeping armpits dry. Many products offer a deodorant/antiperspirant combination.

After a bath or shower, dress yourself in clean clothes. Shirts, socks, and underwear—which can quickly pick up sweaty smells—should be changed daily. This way, both your body and your clothes stay fresh and clean.

Hair

Your hair is one of the first things that people notice about you. The way you wear your hair can say a lot about the way you want to be perceived. Some people like to make a statement by wearing their hair in wild or unconventional styles. They might get mohawks, grow dreadlocks, shave their heads, or dye their hair electric blue. Other teens like to follow the trends. One year it might be cool to have shoulder-length hair. The following year, a buzz cut might be in. Still others have no interest whatsoever in experimenting with their hair. They might keep the same no-nonsense style for years, which is practical and suits them just fine. Ultimately, it doesn't really matter how you choose to wear your hair, as long as it is clean and well cared for.

Different people have different types of hair. Hair can be

Grooming your hair is easy and takes very little time.

thin or thick, strong or brittle, soft or coarse, oily or dry.
When you wash it, you should choose a shampoo and conditioner that suits your type of hair—usually oily, dry, or
normal. People with oily hair need to shampoo frequently,
whereas washing dry hair too often will cause the ends to
split. You may also want to use a conditioner after you
shampoo, especially if your hair is long. Conditioners
make your hair shiny and healthy-looking.

Some people with dry hair also have dry scalps. The dry
skin that flakes off from the scalp is called dandruff.
Dandruff can be uncomfortably itchy. It can also be
embarrassing when it lands on your shirt, particularly a
dark-colored shirt. A number of dandruff-fighting sham-
poos and lotions are available at your drugstore.

17

After washing and towel-drying your hair, it is a good idea to run a brush or comb through it. This will get rid of dead hair and will leave your hair looking neat and healthy. Then you can style your hair. Some people are content with a towel-dried, natural look; others prefer to use a blow dryer, which gives hair volume.

If you don't like the texture of your hair or the way it falls, you can use styling gels, lotions, or sprays. Some will give you a soft hold, which leaves hair moveable and allows it to be styled into a natural shape. Other products offer a strong hold, which leave hair looking stiff, spiky, and/or wet. Gels and sprays allow you to sculpt your hair into different kinds of styles, but remember to go easy on these products. Using too much at one time can make your hair look greasy and unattractive.

Skin

During adolescence, your glands produce oils that leave your skin much shinier than before. This is especially true for your face, neck, shoulders, chest and back. When the pores of your skin get clogged with oil and dirt, sometimes a pimple or blackhead will form.

As annoying as zits may be, take comfort in the fact that about 80 percent of adolescents get them. Sometimes teens develop a more serious skin problem called acne. Acne pimples are very red and sometimes get infected and swollen. Acne is hereditary; teens who get acne usually have a parent who had it. In order to treat acne, it is

Regular showers are an important part of daily grooming.

usually necessary to consult a dermatologist, who can supply you with the proper medication.

Although good grooming won't stop you from getting zits, it can help you to get fewer of them. The surest way to fight against zits is to keep your face clean. Wash your face with mild soap and warm water, then rinse with cool water. There are also special soaps and creams you can use that help control pimples. Ask a pharmacist or dermatologist to recommend one that is appropriate for your skin type.

Although it is often very tempting, try your best not to pop your zits. Not only will they take longer to disappear, but you can be left with a permanent scar.

Shaving

Many guys get excited when they see the first appearance of facial hair. Initially, this hair is quite fine. It usually appears above your upper lip. But over time, it will grow thicker. Hair will also appear along the sides of your face (sideburns) and then around your cheeks, chin and neck.

When you decide to shave for the first time is up to you. It depends on how much hair you have on your face. Some guys think it looks more grown-up to leave their first mustache hairs untouched. Others want to shave them off right away. These days, many guys consider it cool to have a face covered in stubble. However, for many occasions—such as formal events or job interviews—it is appropriate to be clean-shaven.

When you decide you are ready to shave, you can use

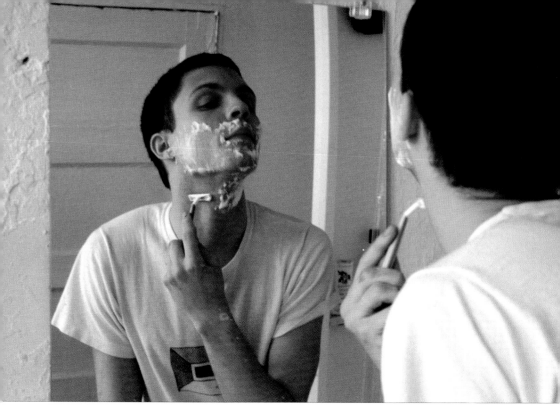

Shaving can irritate sensitive or dry skin, so be sure to use lots of lather.

either an electric razor or a disposable plastic one. If you choose a disposable razor, it is best to shave after taking a shower, when your face is still wet and the hairs are more flexible. Lather your face and neck with shaving cream and then glide the razor across your skin. Be careful, because it is easy to cut yourself. Shaving takes practice. You might want to ask your dad or older brother for some tips.

With an electric razor, you don't need shaving cream, and you can shave with a dry face. Another advantage of an electric razor is that you can't cut yourself.

After shaving, rinse your face with cool water. If desired, splash on a few drops of a soothing, moisturizing aftershave or cologne. This will refresh you and make your skin smell good.

Hands and Fingernails

There are so many activities for which you use your hands. Simply holding a pencil, opening a door, or picking up a telephone can expose hands to dirt and germs. Because your hands also come into frequent contact with your eyes, nose, and mouth, it is extremely important to always keep them clean. If not, you greatly increase the chance of catching a disease.

It is a good idea to wash your hands several times a day, especially after using the bathroom or before handling food. Scrub nails with a nail brush and soap. Then keep them trimmed and groomed with nail clippers or a nail file.

Feet and Toenails

People don't see your feet as often as they see your hands. However, feet are sensitive. Since we rely on them so much, it is important to take care of them. Men's feet sweat a lot, especially when they play sports. After any athletic activity, make sure to wash your feet well, especially in between your toes. When you finish, put on clean socks. Both cotton and wool socks are made of natural fibers that will absorb sweat and allow feet to breathe. Cotton socks are better in the summer, wool ones in the winter. (It is preferable to wear socks made of synthetic fabrics for sports and athletic activities, however, since these fabrics do not absorb sweat and will keep your feet drier.) And it is always a good idea to wear socks with shoes rather

Some basic grooming items are helpful to maintain personal hygiene.

than go barefoot. When you don't wear socks, your feet sweat directly into your shoes, making both your feet and your shoes smell bad.

It's a good idea to wear athletic slippers or flip-flops at a public swimming pool or locker room. If you walk barefoot in such areas, you might catch athlete's foot. This is a fungus that grows between your toes and can become red, itchy and irritated.

Although they aren't generally exposed as often as fingernails are, it is still important to keep toenails clean and trimmed. Use clippers or manicure scissors and cut them straight across. This will help you avoid ingrown toenails, which can be painful.

Mouth and Teeth

Since you were a little kid, you've probably had it drummed into your head to always brush your teeth after meals. This is especially good advice once you hit puberty. As a teenager, hormonal changes affect the acids in your mouth. These in turn can lead to halitosis, or bad breath. Other common sources of bad breath include poor dental hygiene and food with lots of onions or garlic. The best way to keep your mouth clean and fresh-smelling is to brush your teeth after every meal.

Brushing also keeps teeth strong, white, and healthy. Every time you eat, food particles get lodged between your teeth. If you don't brush regularly, they will begin to form plaque, which causes tooth decay. In addition to brushing, you should use dental floss to get at these particles. Regular flossing also prevents gum disease.

Use a toothpaste that contains fluoride, which helps to prevent cavities, and baking soda, which keeps teeth white. And remember, coffee, tea, and cigarettes stain teeth an ugly yellow.

There is no substitute for regular brushing and flossing. Mouthwash, mints, and sugarless gum might temporarily leave your breath smelling fresh, but they won't clean your teeth or get rid of plaque. Always visit a dentist for a checkup and cleaning twice a year. It is worth taking care of your mouth and teeth, because few things are more attractive than a beautiful smile.

Chapter 3

Clothing and You

As the old saying goes, "Clothes make the man." And teenagers—both male and female—discover quickly that what they wear can have a big impact on their lives. Clothing choices affect how you will be treated—and if you will be accepted or respected—by adults and especially your peers.

Other teens can be very critical. They often create their own code of what is cool and what isn't. This can create a tough situation. You want to be accepted, but does that really mean you have to buy $140 basketball shoes? Yet if you show up at school wearing $10 no-name sneakers, you might be laughed at.

There's nothing wrong with wanting to fit in and following trends, as long as you are sure that you really like doing so. Don't be a slave to fashion or to your peers. Try to mix what is considered in with your own

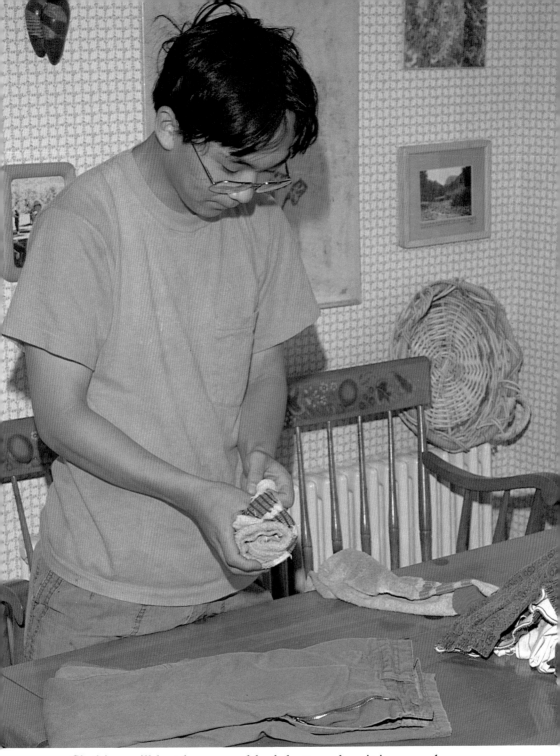
Clothing will last longer and look better when it is properly cared for.

individual tastes, and don't be afraid to experiment with clothes to discover what looks best on you and what makes you feel good.

John didn't care that much about what he wore. He always let his mother buy his back-to-school clothes for him: a couple of pairs of khakis, some cotton button-down shirts, a pair of brown oxfords, and a pair of sneakers. But at the beginning of sophomore year, a really pretty new girl named Selma transferred to his school. John developed a major crush on Selma. He made a point of walking by her locker a lot, but she didn't seem to notice him. He even changed seats in math class so that he could sit closer to her, but she never even glanced his way.

"Find out what Selma thinks about me," he told his friend Sue Ellen, who had become friends with Selma.

"She doesn't even know who you are," reported Sue Ellen.

"How can that be?" asked John. "I sit beside her in math class!"

"John," said Sue Ellen. "The problem is that you look like your mother dresses you."

"She does," replied John.

"Well, that's the problem. You look kind of geeky—always wearing button-down shirts and boring colors. You should wear something that makes more of an impression."

Sue Ellen decided to take John shopping. John tried on lots of different clothes. They discovered that blue brought out the color of his eyes and that looser clothes made him look more relaxed and confident. Instead of khakis and pastel shirts, they chose black jeans and T-shirts. "They're really simple, but cool," said Sue Ellen, evaluating John's new look.

The next morning before school, John put on his new clothes and looked at himself in the mirror. He liked what he saw. He felt more grown-up and happy with himself. Instead of letting his hair lie flat, he combed it back with some gel. He even dabbed on a bit of cologne. "You look so handsome, honey," said John's mom when he came down for breakfast.

At school, a couple of friends complimented him on his new look. John felt so confident that he even worked up the courage to talk to Selma after math class. While they were walking to her locker, he asked her to go to a movie with him—and she said yes!

Seasonal Wear

Obviously, the kinds of clothes you need to buy depend upon the climate in which you live. It is essential to have clothes that are suited to specific seasons or kinds of weather.

In the spring or summer, you will probably need to wear clothing made out of lightweight materials such as cotton or linen. Cotton is a great fabric; its natural fibers keep you cool. It is also soft, comfortable, and durable. Short-sleeved shirts and shorts are ideal for summer months. For more formal occasions, however, long pants are appropriate.

During the fall and winter, choose heavier clothes made out of thicker materials. Once again, natural fibers are best. While protecting you from the cold, they also breathe so that you won't get too hot or sweaty. They also tend to be softer and sturdier than synthetic materials. Wool is great for sweaters, hats, scarves, and socks. Although it must be washed carefully, woolen clothing often has interesting textures. And heavier weaves of cotton, such as flannel and corduroy, are ideal for shirts and pants.

Casual and Formal Events

As you get older, you will discover that specific occasions require specific types of clothing. Sometimes— like when you are at school, the movies, or just hanging out—it is fine to dress in a relaxed, casual style. In fact, if you overdress in such situations, you will probably feel silly and out of place. At other times, however, you will definitely make a bad impression if you show up in clothes that are informal, inappropriate, or sloppy.

When Tony's basketball team won the state championship, Coach decided to celebrate by taking the whole team out to a fancy dinner at a fine restaurant. "Remember, guys—this is a dressy affair," he warned the team.

"What are you going to wear to the dinner?" Tony asked his teammate Muki.

"Well . . . I don't want to get dressed up, but my dad's been to that restaurant before," Muki replied. "He says I should wear a jacket and tie."

Tony couldn't believe it. "C'mon, Mook! It's just going to be the Coach and us. No way am I going to wear any stupid monkey suit!"

The night of the dinner, Tony showed up at the restaurant wearing sneakers and jeans. He looked like he was on his way to basketball practice. When he told the headwaiter that he was there for the team dinner, the headwaiter gave him a cold look and refused to seat him.

"I am sorry, sir," said the headwaiter. "Our patrons are required to wear a jacket and tie."

Some dress codes are obvious. You wouldn't go to a formal dance without wearing a tuxedo or show up at a wedding without a jacket and tie. However, many rules about dress are unwritten. It can be hard sometimes to know exactly which clothes are suitable for a certain situation and which are not. Say you have been invited to a dinner party. How do you know if the dress will be dressy or casual? In such cases, it is always best to find out in advance so that you can dress appropriately. That way, you will avoid any embarrassment.

Shopping

Leon gets miserable every time he has to go shopping for new clothes. Even though he is fifteen, his mother still insists on going with him. It embarrasses Leon to have to go to the young men's section of a department store accompanied by his mother. Also, whenever they go shopping together, Leon and his mother always argue. She criticizes the new and different styles that Leon thinks are cool, saying that he should stick to styles that are more practical and basic.

Leon's mother spends a long time picking out clothes for him to try on. Then she insists that Leon come out of the dressing room so she can see if they fit. In front of the whole store, she yanks on his sleeves and even pulls at the seat of his pants. Once when she did that, two guys from school, Stu and Ben, happened to walk by. Stu and Ben snickered at Leon. He wanted to die.

When Leon and his mother got home, he was so mad about what happened that he yelled at her. She understood that Leon might feel uncomfortable going shopping for clothes with her. At the same time, she didn't think it was a good idea for him to buy all of his own clothes himself. Finally, they came to an agreement. Leon would get a monthly clothing allowance with which he could buy whatever he wanted. But twice a year, his mother would take him to buy back-to-school and summer basics that she thought were necessary.

When shopping for clothes, price is important, but so is quality. Check tags to see what fabric an item of clothing is made of. Also check the washing instructions. Clothes that need to be dry-cleaned are sometimes less practical than clothes that can just be machine-washed.

There are many different places to shop. Department stores are great for looking at a lot of things all at once. If you're looking for something very specific, however,

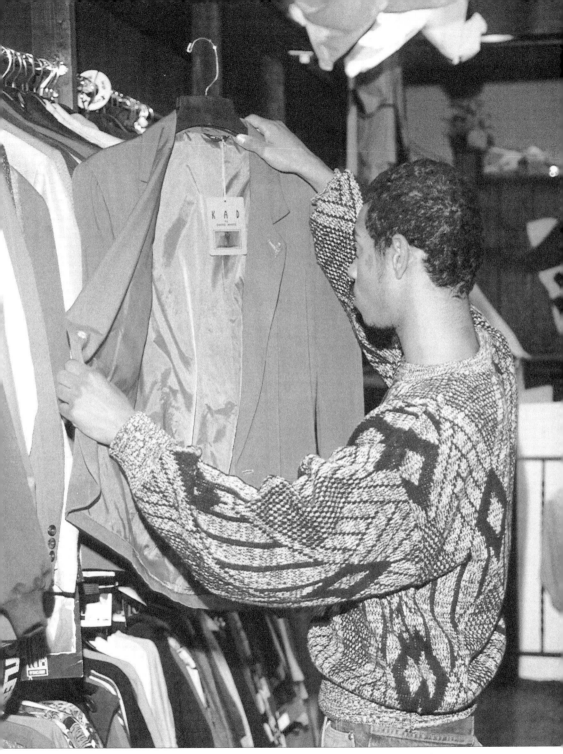
It is wise to examine clothes for quality and durable fabrics as well as style.

you might want to go to a particular boutique. Of course, your budget is an issue. You may want to consider discount stores and second-hand stores. They can be a great source for basics, as well as for the odd funky piece of clothing.

Taking Care of Your Clothes

As you begin to build your wardrobe, it is important to learn how to maintain it. This means keeping your clothes neat, clean, and ironed. Pants, shirts, socks, and underwear should be washed often. Jackets and coats, as well as some sweaters and pants, should be sent to the dry cleaner.

Once a year, go through your entire wardrobe. Remove items that are too small or that you are simply tired of. Make small repairs, such as replacing buttons. Clothes that you have outgrown or won't wear again might be welcomed by a younger relative or friend. Or you could donate your old clothes to a charitable organization or thrift store.

Footwear

Shoes are an important part of your wardrobe, too. Be sure that new shoes fit properly and are comfortable when you try them on.

Most teenagers love sneakers and wear them just about everywhere. Some sneakers have even become a status symbol, and many kids feel that they must pay huge amounts of money for a brand name. But good sneakers don't have to be expensive. You'll be surprised how much prices vary if you shop around and wait for sales.

For variety and for more formal occasions, it is a good idea to have at least a couple of pairs of shoes or boots. In general, it is best to choose a standard color and style that will go with most of your clothes. Black and dark brown are the most practical. Most boots and shoes need polishing in order to look shiny and to stay supple. Pay attention to signs of wear. Shoes and boots can also be resoled or reheeled to look almost new.

Chapter 4

Getting in Shape

*A*very hated sports. He especially hated gym class. Because he was overweight, he got tired quickly and couldn't run very fast. The other guys called him "Chubs" and "Porkchop" and were always making jokes about him. Whenever they had to divide into teams, Avery was the last guy picked. He felt like a big loser.

When he began his junior year, Avery was relieved. Finally, gym class was no longer obligatory—no more feeling like an uncoordinated geek. Unfortunately, however, gym class had been the only place where Avery ever got any exercise. Once he no longer had to take it, he began to gain even more weight.

That winter, Avery's dad had a heart attack. Like Avery, his dad was overweight. Like Avery, his dad ate a lot of fatty foods and frequently snacked between *meals. Like Avery, his dad barely ever exercised. And Avery's dad was young—only forty-three years old.*

"This heart attack was a warning," his dad said when he came home from the hospital. "For me—but also for you, son. You and I are going to change our ways and get fit."

Avery's mother and father consulted a nutritionist and learned how to prepare lighter, healthier meals. Avery's father went to the local gym and got a year-long membership for the whole family. The gym was on the way home from Avery's school, so it was very convenient for him. And because it was open at night and on weekends, Avery could go any time he wanted.

Although he had always hated team sports, Avery discovered that there were many individual activities he could do at the gym. He loved to swim and he found weight lifting to be energizing. He and his dad also decided to take up racquetball together. At first, they were both pretty bad. But after a few weeks, their game improved. By springtime, Avery was able to play in the intramural racquetball champion-ships—and he came in third. He had never felt so good about himself.

Within a few months, Avery was able to run fast without getting out of breath. He was losing weight and his body was becoming firm and toned. For the first time ever, he started to like his body.

In the beginning, it's always difficult to start any kind of exercise program. It's even more difficult to stick to

Exercising on a regular basis will help you feel and look better.

it. Reasons such as "I'm too tired today," "I don't have enough time," or "Exercise is boring," are common excuses. Try picking an activity you really like that fits easily into your schedule. Maybe you would prefer to work out with a friend or participate in a team activity. Whatever you choose to do, remember that exercise is essential to the way you look and feel.

Choosing an Activity

There is an almost endless range of exercises and activities that you can do to keep physically fit. It is most important to choose something that you like. Consider the demands of various sports and how well your body is equipped to deal with them. Basketball might be difficult if you're five-foot-three—but you could use your height to great advantage on the soccer field.

For some people, team sports are ideal. Regular games and practices ensure that you get lots of exercise. Playing with and against other teens can be both hard work and a lot of fun. Sports such as baseball, football, volleyball, and basketball foster cooperation and a sense of team spirit. The competitive nature of these sports can be a great source of motivation as well.

Other people are more comfortable with or interested in individual sports. These activities can help you to develop personal skills such as self-motivation and self-discipline. Outside of school, it is easier to fit some individual sports and exercises—such as rowing, running, weight lifting, or in-line skating—into a busy schedule.

Because you can jump rope, run, or ride your bike at any time and almost anywhere, these exercises allow you much more flexibility. Dance—from ballet to break-dancing—is another great activity. So are yoga, tai chi, karate, and skateboarding. Even taking a long, fast walk a few times a week can keep you healthy and in shape.

Physical Benefits of Exercise

A regular fitness routine benefits the body in many ways. Exercise helps you to maintain a proper weight by lowering the body's fat level, replacing fat with lean muscle mass.

It also increases the body's release of chemicals called endorphins. Endorphins act as a natural pain-killer and relaxant, helping to improve your mood. Also, regular exercise causes the oxygen level in the brain to increase. This is believed to aid creativity and also plays a role in preventing illness.

It may surprise you to learn that exercise will increase, rather than decrease, your energy level. Regular exercise allows you to do more without becoming tired. You will sleep better at night and feel more rested in the morning.

With any physical activity, your heart pumps more blood to various parts of the body. This not only increases the strength of the various organs, but also strengthens the heart itself. Blood vessels—the arteries and veins—increase in size to allow more blood to flow to and from the heart. Endurance levels increase, providing more energy during the course of the day.

Fitness can have a positive impact on your physical health. It can have a strong impact on your mental health as well. When your body looks good and you feel healthy, you feel better about yourself as a person. Your self-acceptance and self-confidence increases. You feel better able to achieve your goals.

Psychological Benefits of Exercise

As you know, things that affect your body affect your mind, and vice-versa. Therefore, it is not surprising that exercise can have many positive effects on your state of mind.

As your physical condition improves, so does your self-esteem. High self-esteem helps you to handle problems and stress. Sticking to a specific exercise schedule will also make you a more committed and self-motivated person. Regular exercise will likely make you more calm and relaxed. The same endurance and determination that physical exertion requires can be used to help you cope with difficult situations.

Exercise provides a great outlet for releasing negative thoughts and energies in a positive way. It helps you look at life from a more balanced and less critical perspective.

Chapter 5

Eating Well

Food and water are the basic necessities of life. Eating properly allows our bodies to grow and become stronger. As you grow older and begin to cook for yourself or eat more frequently outside of your home, it is important to understand proper nutrition.

You probably enjoy eating candy, soda, ice cream, and other sweet foods and beverages. Not only do they taste good, many provide a quick shot of energy known as a "sugar high." However, because they also contain large amounts of sugar and sometimes fat, these foods can cause serious health problems, especially when consumed in large amounts. Eating foods that are high in sugar, fat, and/or salt quickly adds unwanted pounds. Equally unhealthy when eaten regularly are deep-fried foods. Long-term effects of a poor diet can include cavities, diabetes, high blood pressure, and heart disease.

Eating a well-balanced diet and drinking plenty of water are essential for good health.

Make a healthy, balanced diet part of your lifestyle. It is particularly important to drink lots of water— at least eight glasses a day—and to eat many fruits and vegetables. (Among its many benefits, drinking lots of water is great for your skin.) Remember that diet and exercise are both essential to maintain a positive body image.

Eating Right

The foods that we eat are made up of proteins, carbohydrates, fats, fiber, and various nutrients. Most foods contain a variety of vitamins and minerals that are needed for a healthy body. There are many foods for you to choose from to develop and maintain a healthy body. If you eat properly and in moderation, you should receive all the vitamins and minerals your body needs.

It is important to eat three solid meals a day. Eating breakfast is essential. The vitamins and energy that you receive from a good breakfast will really jump-start your day. Not only will you feel better, but studies show thst students who eat breakfast perform better at school.

No matter how busy you are, don't skip meals. It is okay to grab a burger and fries once in a while if you are pressed for time, but don't make it a habit.

Bad Habits

Whenever Ernie walks into the kitchen, he heads to the fridge. It's an automatic reaction—even when he's not hungry, he opens the door and checks out what is inside. Before closing the door, he almost always grabs something—a chicken leg, a piece of pie, a handful of olives— and eats it on the spot. His girlfriend Charysse can't figure out why Ernie has gotten so chubby lately. Actually, neither can Ernie. Opening the refrigerator and reaching inside for something has become such a casual action for Ernie that he doesn't even think of it as eating.

For some people, eating becomes a habit, just like turning on the televsion out of boredeom. Don't snack if you're not really hungry. When you eat, sit down and take your time. And don't ever eat until you feel ready

When you are hungry, sit down and take your time to eat.

to explode. Not only will you feel sick to your stomach, but this also is a sure way to gain weight. If there is too much food on your plate, simply wrap it up and save it for another meal.

Obesity

Obesity means being very overweight—at least 20 percent above the maximum recommended weight for one's height. Being obese limits one's activities and places great strain on the body. Obesity can lead to serious medical problems and contribute to poor mental health as well. Obese people are often made fun of and may have very low self-esteem as a result.

Although obesity is not that common among teens, there are more overweight adolescents in North America today than ever before. In the last thirty years, the number of overweight kids in the United States has more than doubled. Today, approximately one out of five kids between the ages of six and seventeen is considered overweight. And studies show that most fat kids become fat adults. Recent statistics reveal that 37 percent (100 million) of Americans are overweight—and 30 million are obese.

Even if you are only slightly overweight, it is a good idea to start exercising and watching your diet now. Being overweight can cause high blood pressure, respiratory problems, and some forms of cancer. Establishing a fit lifestyle at an early age will help you to fight fatness throughout the rest of your life.

Dieting

There is a tremendous amount of information available about dieting and weight loss. Unfortunately, most diets don't work, and some are downright dangerous. For a diet to be healthy and successful, it must meet three conditions:

1. It must be sensible. This means eating the right kinds of food in the proper proportions. If you must snack, choose raw vegetables and fruit.
2. It must be accompanied by regular exercise. This means working out for thirty to forty minutes, three to five times a week. Your goal is to turn the stored fat into muscle. You can do this through exercise.
3. You must be disciplined enough to stick to conditions 1 and 2. It may help to participate in a support group, but at some point you need to take charge yourself.

People who go on diets often talk a great deal about vitamins and special food supplements. Keep in mind, however, that most of the vitamins and minerals you need can be found in a well-balanced, healthy diet.

You may want to see your doctor before going on a diet. A good diet involves making sensible choices about what you eat and when you eat, and eating food in smaller portions. Have realistic expectations and expect weight loss to happen gradually.

Chapter 6

A Healthy Outlook

Ahealthy lifestyle means taking care of your body so that you look and feel the best that you possibly can. But how you perceive yourself—and how others perceive you—is based not simply on your exterior but on your interior as well. Just as important as developing a healthy body is cultivating a healthy outlook on life.

A healthy outlook or attitude includes many things. It means focusing on positive aspects of your personality, while working to combat your shortcomings. It means developing self-confidence and feeling good about yourself. It means treating yourself and those around you with kindness and respect. And it means trying your best to look at situations in the most positive light possible. Just as someone with a healthy body and a good sense of style impresses others, so does someone with an engaging personality and a positive attitude.

Self-Control

Life today is filled with many pressures. You may often feel pressured by your parents, teachers, and peers. Such stress can frequently cause you to be nervous or anxious.

When life gets really stressful, some teens become upset and lose control of their emotions. They may resort to extreme behavior, such as yelling, throwing things, or punching someone. But someone with a strong sense of self and a healthy attitude toward life will probably be better at maintaining control in a stressful situation.

What about you? What do you do when things get tough? Do you stay calm and try to think clearly? Or do you tend to blow up and strike out at everyone and everything around you?

When Mr. Pivnicki handed the math midterm back to his students, both Dirk and Mario were shocked to discover that they had received failing grades.

"Aw, man!" yelled Dirk, slapping his hand down on his desk. "I can't believe this!" Everyone in the class turned to look at him. "Hey, Pivnicki!" he shouted.

Mr. Pivnicki cut Dirk off. "If you have a problem with your grade, Dirk, you can talk to me about it after class," he said calmly.

Dirk was irritated by Mr. Pivnicki's tone. He stood up, knocking his chair onto the floor behind him.

"Sit down, Dirk," warned Mr. Pivnicki. "I won't stand for this behavior."

"Oh yeah?" shouted Dirk. He gave Mr. Pivnicki the finger and stormed out of the classroom, slamming the door behind him.

Mario was just as upset by his failing grade. When he saw the mark in red ink, he closed his eyes and took a deep breath. Mario's mind was racing. He couldn't concentrate during the rest of the class period because he was trying to think of a way not to fail the entire course. Perhaps Mr. Pivnicki would let him take a make-up test. Or maybe he could do an extra assignment. Mario made a mental list of his options. He tried to stay calm until he could talk to Mr. Pivnicki after class.

Maintaining self-control can take a lot of practice. Sometimes it seems as if you won't be able to hold your emotions in check. But you may be surprised at how much control you actually have.

In almost all situations, it is better to calm down and think rationally rather than act on the spur of the moment. Start by focusing on the positive. Take deep breaths. Try to put difficult situations in their proper perspective. Don't let minor irritations get to you.

Assertiveness

Being assertive involves self-confidence; it suggests that you expect the people around you to treat you with the same respect that you have for yourself.

Assertiveness isn't about showing disrespect for others, but it is about having the courage to honestly say what's on your mind and stand up for what you believe is right. Do you speak up when you know a wrong has been committed? When you try to correct an unjust situation, you are acting assertively.

Don't confuse assertiveness with aggressiveness. Aggressive people tend to think that they can solve problems by resorting to verbal or physical threats. Nothing could be further from the truth. Although they may scare some people into doing what they want, nobody likes a bully. And those who are unable to control aggressive behavior will have a lot of difficulty getting along with people. They can even get themselves into serious trouble.

Manners

Another important part of a healthy outlook is having good manners. Treating people with respect, kindness, and politeness is an essential part of being a decent human being. When you meet people for the first time, your manners have a very strong impact on how they perceive you and how they will treat you in return.

Mr. and Mrs. Schmidt and their son Gray planned to spend the first weekend in spring at their cottage in the woods. "Why don't you invite a couple of your friends, Gray?" suggested Mrs. Schmidt. Gray asked his two new buddies from the ski team, Tim and Griffin. Mr. and

Mrs. Schmidt had never met either boy before. But once they were all at the cottage, Gray's parents got to know Tim and Griffin quickly.

On Saturday morning, Mrs. Schmidt found Tim making a big stack of pancakes in the kitchen. "Good morning, Mrs. Schmidt. Hope the noise didn't wake you," he said. After breakfast, Tim helped clear the table before offering to help Gray and Mr. Schmidt chop some wood for the fireplace.

Griffin, on the other hand, didn't get up until noon. "Hey," he said to Mrs. Schmidt when he came into the living room, yawning and scratching his head. "Got anything to eat?" While Mrs. Schmidt made him a late breakfast, Griffin decided to take a bath. By the time he came out of the bathroom, the food Mrs. Schmidt had made was cold. Griffin sat down and shoveled the food down as if he hadn't eaten in three days.

Later, while the three boys were walking in the woods, Mrs. Schmidt walked by the guest bedroom. Tim's bed was neatly made and his clothes were folded on a chair. Griffin's bed was unmade and his clothes were strewn messily on top of his sheets.

On Sunday evening, the Schmidts dropped Tim and Griffin off at their homes. "Thanks so much, Mr. and Mrs. Schmidt. I had a really great time," Tim said as he got out of the car, smiling warmly. When the Schmidts pulled up in Griffin's driveway, Griffin got out of the car and slammed the door. "See you guys later," he yelled over his shoulder as he ran up the drive to his house.

Guess whose manners made a better impression on Mr. and Mrs. Schmidt—Tim's, or Griffin's. And guess who will get asked back to the cottage—and who won't.

Treating Yourself Well

While this book stresses the importance of treating others well, you must not overlook the importance of being good to yourself.

At times you are bound to be in situations and relationships that are frustrating and negative. It can be easy to blame yourself for things that aren't going right. Even though it might be difficult, try focusing on your positive traits during those times when you feel like a failure. Everybody has bad days and even bad weeks. At these times, it is important to treat yourself well.

Make yourself feel better by offering yourself small treats or pleasures that you really enjoy. Rent a favorite video, ride your bike somewhere you've never been, go out and take some photos, or visit a good friend you haven't seen in a while. Just try to relax and remember that nothing stays bad forever.

Ultimately, you have no control over the actions of those around you. But you do have control over yourself. If you think positively and be the best you can be, you'll usually find that others will respond the same way.

Chapter 7

Putting It All Together

In the introduction, we met Raphael, whose lifestyle was growing increasingly unhealthy. Because Raphael didn't take good care of himself, those around him began to respond negatively to him. This made Raphael have an even more negative attitude about himself. Physically, he neglected himself; psychologically, he felt depressed, unloved, and not confident.

When Raphael got arrested and suspended for marijuana use, he hit bottom. He was forced to change his ways—because he was ordered to attend a counseling program. He took a good hard look at himself and didn't like what he saw. With the support of his counselor, Raphael decided to start taking better care of himself. It was time for him to make changes toward a healthier lifestyle.

Raphael had a long talk with his mom, and they

worked out an agreement. Raphael would do work around the house—cooking meals, keeping things clean, mowing the lawn, and raking leaves—and in return his mother would give him a monthly allowance. Raphael liked feeling responsible for the house. It made him feel grown-up and needed. It also gave him money to buy some cool new clothes.

Because he was now busy doing things around the house, Raphael no longer had the time to sit around and watch television. He also didn't feel like eating junk food—especially once he started the cooking course that his mom gave him as a birthday present. Raphael liked cooking class a lot. He really got into making food and sharing it with his mom. Soon, he decided to quit smoking. Cigarettes prevented him from fully appreciating the taste and smell of the dishes he prepared.

To get to cooking class, Raphael rode an old bike he bought at a garage sale. He loved zooming around town, and soon noticed that his body began to feel a lot more alive. Raphael started biking everywhere he went. Before long, he had lost a little weight. He started to feel good about his body and had a lot more energy.

At cooking school, he met Shane, who was a guitarist. Shane was putting together a funk group. When he found out that Raphael was a drummer, he asked him to join the band. Raphael found it really satisfying to be playing music again. It was as if a big part of himself that he had lost had been rediscovered.

Instead of tiring him out, all of these activities

helped to keep Raphael focused. He was better able to concentrate at school, and his grades began to improve. Doing so many things he cared about made him feel good about himself and made him more extroverted. He noticed that the kids at school were no longer avoiding him—they were now much friendlier. He in turn was friendly back.

Raphael's life isn't perfect. He still wants to lose a little more weight, and he gets zits every so often. He'll probably have to go to summer school to make up for two failed subjects. But his new lifestyle makes him feel much better. If he keeps it up, life will get better still.

Glossary

acceptance Approval; favorable reception by one's peers.

acne A skin disorder that causes pimples on the face.

athlete's foot An itchy foot fungus often found between the toes.

blackhead A pimple that results when a gland becomes clogged with oil, turning black when exposed to air.

commitment Pledging or promising yourself to a course of action.

dandruff Tiny flakes of dry scalp.

dental floss A thread used to remove food particles.

dermatologist A doctor who specializes in treating skin disorders.

dreadlocks A hairstyle of long, braided or matted strands of hair.

endorphins   Chemical substances released in the body that reduce stress and promote a sense of well-being.

fluoride   A chemical found in drinking water and toothpaste that keeps teeth strong.

halitosis   The medical term for bad breath.

hygiene   Practices that promote health, such as cleanliness.

mohawk   A hairstyle with a narrow center strip of spiky hair and the sides shaved.

plaque   A sticky film that forms on the surface of teeth and can lead to decay.

pores   Tiny openings in the skin.

tai chi   Ancient Chinese meditation exercises.

trendy   Something that is fashionable or stylish; usually refers to clothing and hairstyles.

yoga   A system of exercises aimed at producing mental and spiritual well-being.

For Further Reading

Akagi, Cynthia G. *Dear Michael: Sexuality Education for Boys Ages 11–17*. Littleton, CO: Gylantic Publishing Co., 1994.

Blume, Judy. *Then Again, Maybe I Won't* (reissued ed.). Boston: G.K. Hall, 1988.

Bourgeois, Paulette and Martin Wolfish. *Changes in You and Me: A Book About Puberty, Mostly for Boys.* Kansas City: Andrews and McMeel, 1994.

Daldray, Jeremy. *Boys Behaving Badly: The Teenage Guy's Survival Guide.* New York: Little, Brown & Co., 1999.

Figtree, Dale. *Eat Smart: A Guide to Good Health for Kids.* Clinton, NJ: New Win Publishing, 1997.

Glassman, Bruce S. *Everything You Need to Know About Growing Up Male* (rev ed.). New York: Rosen Publishing, 1997.

Graff, Cynthia Stamper. *Bodypride: An Action Plan for Teens—Seeking Self-Esteem and Building Better Bodies.* Glendale, CA: Griffin Publishing, 1997.

Gravelle, Karen. *What's Going on Down There: Answers to Questions Boys Find Hard to Ask.* New York: Walker and Co., 1998.

Gurian, Michael. *From Boys to Men: All About Adolescence and You.* New York: Price Stern Sloan Publishing, 1999.

McCoy, Kathy and Charles Wibblesman. *The New Teenage Body Book* (rev. ed.). New York: Body Press/Perigee, 1992.

Where to Go for Help

Web Sites

Diet and Weight Loss/Fitness Home Page
http://www.mhv.net/~donn/diet.html
Diet and nutrition tips for teens.

Teen.com
http://www.teen.com
This site covers all types of teen issues.

On-Line Magazines

BLAST!
http://www.blastmag.com/main.html

React.com
http://www.react.com

Teenzine
http://members.xoom.com/tznet

Men's Health/Fitness Magazines

Men's Fitness
http://www.fitnessonline.com/mensfitness

Men's Health
http://www.menshealth.com/new/issue/index.html

Fitness and Health Associations

In the United States

YMCA of the USA
101 North Wacker Drive
Chicago, IL 60606
(312) 977-0031
Web site: http://www.ymca.net

In Canada

YMCA Canada
42 Charles Street East, 6th Floor
Toronto, Ontario
M4Y 1T4
(416) 967-9622
Web site: http://www.ymca.ca/home.htm

Index

About the Author

Michael A. Sommers is a writer/journalist with a graduate degree in History and Civilizations, a sister named Annie, and a cat named Jesse.

Photo Credits

Cover photo by Simca Israelian. Pp. 12, 17, 21, 43 by Simca Israelian; all other photos by Stuart Rabinowitz